# Pick Up Lines

## Chat Up Your Dream Girl

R. J. Clarke

# Pick Up Lines

**M:** I thought that happiness started with a H but now I know it starts with U

**M:** Do you believe in love at first sight or should I walk by again?

**M:** If you stood in front of a mirror with 11 roses, you would see 12 of the most beautiful things in the world

**M:** Hi, my friends over there said that I couldn't start a conversation with the most beautiful girl in this bar. Do you want to buy some drinks with their money?

**M:** Of all the beautiful curves on your body, your smile is my favorite

**M:** Is that the sun rising or is that just you brightening up my world?

**M:** Hi, I thought I'd come over and say hello before you caught me staring

**M:** Hi, I'm Mr. Right - I heard you were looking for me

**M:** Can you pull this heart-shaped arrow out of my butt?
**F:** What arrow?
**M:** The one that a little kid with wings shot me with

**M:** Can I borrow a kiss, I promise I will give it back?

**M:** I just noticed you noticing me and I just wanted to give you notice that I noticed you too

**M:** Excuse me; I think you have something in your eye.
**F:** I don't feel anything there
**M:** My mistake, it's just a sparkle

**M:** Did you see the rainbow today?
**F:** No I must have missed it
**M:** I think I have found the treasure at the end of the rainbow

**M:** I love your freckles. I think a woman without them is like a night without stars

**M:** If nothing lasts forever, will you be my nothing?

**M:** If it was zero degrees in here, you would still move me

**M:** God gave us two ears, two eyes, two legs and two arms but he only gave us one heart. I believe that God wanted me to find you so that I can give you another heart

**M:** You must be a magician because when I look at you, everything else disappears

**M:** Do you want to play a game?
**F:** Yeah sure, what have you in mind?
**M:** Anything as long as it isn't hide and seek because a girl like you is impossible to find

**M:** Have you ever been asked out by a raisin?
**F:** No
**M:** How about a date?

**M:** Are you Andy's girlfriend?
**F:** No
**M:** Sorry, Andy told me that he was dating the most beautiful girl in the world, so I assumed it was you

**M:** I may not be a genie but I can make your dreams come true

**M:** Can you catch?
**F:** Yes, why?
**M:** Because I think I am falling for you

**M:** If you were a taser, you would be set on stunning

**M:** Giant polar bear!
**F:** What?
**M:** I just wanted to say something to break the ice

**M:** If I had a dollar for every time I thought of you, I would have a dollar because you never leave my mind

**M:** You're so beautiful that you made me forget my pickup line

**M:** You must be in the wrong place – the Miss Universe contest is over there

**M:** Do you have the telephone number for the Ordinance Survey?
**F:** No, why do you ask?
**M:** Because I wanted to tell them that I found a sight of outstanding natural beauty

**M:** You must be the cure for Alzheimer's because you are unforgettable

**M:** Is there an airport nearby or is that just my heart taking off?

**M:** Do you have the time?
**F:** It's midnight
**M:** No, I mean do you have the time to write down my number?


**M:** Are you a magnet because I am attracted to you?


**M:** When I first saw you, I looked for a signature because every masterpiece has one


**M:** Were you arrested earlier?
**F:** No
**M:** You should have been because it has to be illegal to look that good


**M:** I've lost that loving feeling; will you help me to find it?


**M:** You're so hot, I'll need oven gloves


**M:** Could you please step away from the bar, you're making all of the ice melt


**M:** Are you my appendix?
**F:** Why are you asking such a silly question?
**M:** Because I have a funny feeling in my stomach that I should take you out

**M:** Excuse me, but I think you owe me a drink.
**F:** Why?
**M:** Because when I looked at you from across the room, I dropped mine

**M:** You're the only girl I'll love now but in another ten years, I'll love another girl. She'll call you mommy

**M:** You look really familiar... did we take a class together?
**F:** I don't think so
**M:** I could have sworn we had chemistry

**M:** Do you have a map?
**F:** Not on me, why?
**M:** I am getting lost in your eyes

**M:** See my friend over there. He wants to know if you think I'm cute

**M:** You look a lot like my first wife?
**F:** Really, how many times have you married?
**M:** Oh, I'm still a bachelor

**M:** Are you Google?
**F:** No
**M:** The reason I'm asking is because you are everything I have been searching for

**M:** There's only one thing I would want to change about you and that's your last name

**M:** You must be from Tennessee because you are the only 10 I see

**M:** There is something wrong with my cell phone.
**F:** What's wrong?
**M:** It doesn't have your number in it

**M:** Are your parents bakers?
**F:** No, why?
**M:** Because they sure made you a cutie pie

**M:** I was wondering if you could give me some directions?
**F:** Where to?
**M:** To your heart

**M:** Can I take a picture of you to prove that angels do exist?

**M:** I'm not a photographer but I can picture me and you together

**M:** Was that an earthquake or did you just rock my world?

**M:** Are you an alien?
**F:** Definitely not, why?
**M:** Because you are out of this world

**M:** Haven't I seen you on the front cover of Vogue?

**M:** Your last name must be Gillette because you look like the best a man can get

**M:** You must be a broom because you have just swept me off my feet

**M:** Life without you would be like a broken pencil... pointless

**M:** Did you get your license suspended for driving all these men crazy?

**M:** I think I'm invisible. Can you see me?
**F:** Yes
**M:** How about tomorrow night?

**M:** If looks could kill, you would be a weapon of mass destruction

**M:** If you were a vegetable, you'd be a cute cumber

**M:** Was your dad a king?
**F:** No
**M:** He must have been to make a princess like you


**M:** Hello, I'm doing a survey of what people think are the cheesiest pick up lines. So, do you pick, "Do you come here often?", "What's your sign?" or "Hello, I'm doing a survey of what people think are the cheesiest pick up lines?"


**M:** Hey, do you want to dance, just smile for yes and do a backflip for no


**M:** I'm no organ donor but I would happily give you my heart


**M:** A boy gives a girl 11 real roses and 1 fake rose and says, "I will love you until the last rose dies"


**M:** If you were a chicken, you'd be impeccable


**M:** Grab your coat, you've pulled


**M:** Do you have a twin sister?
**F:** Not that I'm aware of
**M:** Then you must be the most beautiful girl in the world

**M:** For a moment I thought I had died and gone to Heaven. Now I see that I am very much alive and that Heaven has been brought to me

**M:** What time do you have to be back in Heaven?

**M:** Is your name Wi-Fi?
**F:** No
**M:** I'm only asking because I think I feel a connection

**M:** Besides this one, what's the worst pick up line you have ever heard?

**M:** There must be something wrong with my eyes because I can't take them off you

**M:** If you were a burger at McDonalds, you'd be McGorgeous

**M:** You're so beautiful, you've probably heard every chat up line in the book

**M:** I just read the label on your dress and it was just as I thought – made in Heaven

**M:** Your eyes are the same color as my Porsche

**M:** I was blinded by your beauty so I need your name and number for insurance purposes

**M:** On a scale of 1 to 10, you are a 9 and I am the 1 you need

**M:** If I hired 100 artists for 100 years, they still wouldn't be able to paint a picture as beautiful as you

**M:** They say that dating is a numbers game so can I get your number?

**M:** I think that when God made you, he was showing off

**M:** I like the diamonds you are wearing, they are flawless, just like you

**M:** They say that kissing is the language of love so how about a conversation?

**M:** I bet you are an artist because you are drawing my attention

**M:** When I see you, my heart races and I am hoping to win first place

**M:** I hope you know CPR because you take my breath away

**M:** I know somebody who likes you but if I wasn't so shy, I'd tell you who

**M:** Who stole the stars from the sky and put them in your eyes?

**M:** If I could rearrange the alphabet, I would put U and I together

**M:** Pinch me?
**F:** What for?
**M:** Because you're so fine that I must be dreaming

**M:** Do you know what's on the menu?
**F:** No, sorry
**M:** Me-N-U

**M:** I think you have just dropped something?
**F:** What is it?
**M:** My jaw

**M:** Do you work at Starbucks?
**F:** I used to, why do you ask?
**M:** Because I like you a latte

**M:** Are your feet tired?
**F:** Not really, why do you ask?
**M:** Because you have been running around in my mind all day


**M:** Hi, my name is Robert but you can call me tonight


**M:** Your lips look so lonely… would they like to meet mine?


**M:** Your hands look heavy, would you like me to hold them for you?


**M:** I seem to have lost my number, can I borrow yours?


**M:** Can you pass me the tartar sauce because you are quite the catch?


**M:** No wonder the sky is so grey, all of the blue is in your eyes


**M:** Is it hot in here or is it just you?


**M:** You're a piece of eye candy and I have a sweet tooth

**M:** Did it hurt?
**F:** Did what hurt?
**M:** When you fell down from heaven?


**M:** Do you know what this shirt is made from?
**F:** Cotton?
**M:** Boyfriend material


**M:** You must be a snowflake because you truly are one of a kind


**M:** Did we just share electrons because I'm feeling a covalent bond between us


**M:** I think I need to call Heaven because they've lost one of their angels


**M:** Are you religious because you are the answer to all of my prayers


**M:** Your eyes are a mystery and I'd like to be your detective


**M:** Would you like me to buy you an island?


**M:** I bet you play soccer because you're a keeper

**M:** If I said that you had a beautiful body, would you hold it against me?

**M:** Is that a mirror in your pocket?
**F:** No, why?
**M:** Because I can see myself in your pants

**M:** My magic watch says that you are not wearing any underwear
**F:** You're wrong
**M:** Oh, it must be an hour too fast

**M:** Nice legs, what time do they open?

**M:** Hi, can I buy you several drinks?

**M:** Do you know what would be fantastic on you?
**F:** What?
**M:** Me

**M:** You might want to put your crash helmet on tonight
**F:** Why?
**M:** Because you are going through the head board

**M:** How about you sit on my lap and we'll talk about the first thing that pops up?

**M:** I like mathematics. Do you want to go to my room, add the bed, subtract the clothes, divide the legs and multiply?

**M:** Sarah, do you want to have sex with me?
**F:** My name is not Sarah
**M:** That wasn't the question I was asking

**M:** The word of the day is legs. Let's go back to my place and spread the word

**M:** I think it is time for someone to tell you what everyone is saying behind your back.
**F:** Tell me?
**M:** Nice ass!

**M:** Would you sleep with a stranger?
**F:** No
**M:** Then please allow me to introduce myself

**M:** You know how some men buy expensive cars to make up for certain shortages?
**F:** Yes
**M:** Well, I don't even own a car

**M:** You're like my little toe; small, cute and there's a good chance that I'll bang it on every piece of furniture when I get home

**M:** How do you like your eggs in the morning, scrambled or fertilized?

**M:** Are you a farmer?
**F:** No, why?
**M:** Because you sure know how to raise a cock

**M:** Are you cold?
**F:** No
**M:** You should be because you've been naked in my mind all night

**M:** Smile, if you want to have sex with me

**M:** Are you my new boss?
**F:** I don't think so
**M:** Well, you have just given me a raise

**M:** Don't you think that men that use pick-up lines are dipsticks?
**F:** Yes
**M:** In that case, do you mind if I check your oil level

**M:** Is that a ladder in your tights or is it a stairway to heaven?

**M:** Are you in to casual sex or should I dress up?

**M:** There are 206 bones in the human body. Would you like 207?

**M:** What has 50 teeth and holds back a monster?
**F:** I don't know
**M:** My zipper

**M:** First, I'd like to kiss you passionately on your lips, then I'd like to move up to your belly button

**M:** Are you Medusa?
**F:** No, why?
**M:** Because I'm rock hard

**M:** There's a big sale in my bedroom tonight. Clothes are 100% off

**M:** Do you work at Subway?
**F:** No, why?
**M:** Because you just gave me a footlong

**M:** That dress looks nice but I think it would look better on my bedroom floor

**M:** Do you have any Irish in you?
**F:** No
**M:** Would you like some?

**M:** What's the difference between a Ferrari and an erection?
**F:** I don't know
**M:** I don't have a Ferrari


**M:** I was feeling a little off today but when I saw you, I started to feel turned on


**M:** Did you sit on a pile of sugar
**F:** No, why?
**M:** Because your ass looks pretty sweet


**M:** I'll buy you dinner if you make me breakfast


**M:** I like every bone in your body, especially mine


**M:** I'm jealous of your dress
**F:** Why?
**M:** Because it is touching your body and I'm not


**M:** Do you know what the speed limit of sex is?
**F:** No
**M:** It's 68 because at 69, you have to turn around


**M:** What's better than roses on a piano?
**F:** I don't know
**M:** Tulips on an organ

**M:** Have you had a shower lately because you look like a dirty girl?


**M:** Are you a zoo because you bring out the animal out of me


**M:** If I were to flip a coin, what is the chance that I would get head?


**M:** Let's do breakfast tomorrow. Should I call you or nudge you?

# Funny Pick Up Line Comebacks

**M:** I really want to get into your pants
**F:** No thanks. I already have one asshole in there


**M:** Do you want to see something swell?
**F:** Yeah, where would you like me to punch you?


**M:** You make my software turn into hardware
**F:** I'll make it crash if you're not careful


**M:** Bond. James Bond
**F:** Off. Piss off


**M:** Girl, what's your sign?
**F:** Stop


**M:** Baby, I'm no Fred Flintstone but I can make your bed rock
**F:** I am not a baby and I don't sleep in a cradle

# Tips For Using Pick Up Lines

**Smile.** This will make you look friendlier, approachable and more attractive.

**Maintain eye contact.** This is a powerful way to create an intimate bond. However, try not to stare because it can look a bit creepy.

**Approach confidently.** Stand tall, look at her and try not to trip up over anything – but if you do, laugh it off.

**Choose an appropriate pick up line.** Clean, funny and complimentary pick up lines are the best ones to use to initiate a conversation. Be aware that popular pick up lines aren't going to be funny to someone that has heard them a million times before. Sexual pick up lines rarely work because it shows a woman that you are only interested in one thing. You are also more likely to get a slap, a drink thrown in your face or a knee in your crotch – ouch!

**Speak clearly.** It is very important that she hears what you say. So don't speak too fast, quietly or slur any of your words.

**Make sure that you have something to say afterwards.** This will ensure that there isn't an awkward silence throughout your conversation. It is also important to listen because a woman loves a guy that takes an interest in what they say.

**Good luck out there!**

Printed in Great
Britain
by Amazon